GRANITEWARE

GRANITEWARE
Identification & Value Guide

By Fred and Rose Booher

COLLECTOR BOOKS
A Division of Schroeder Publishing Co., Inc.

Additional copies of this book may be ordered from:

COLLECTOR BOOKS
P.O. Box 3009
Paducah, Kentucky 42001
@ $7.95 Postpaid

Copyright: Fred Booher & Bill Schroeder, 1977
ISBN: 0-89145-067-X

ABOUT THE AUTHORS

Fred and Rose Booher are a husband and wife team, with a background covering many years experience as licensed antique dealers and collectors of American antiques.

Their experience runs through the various activities attendant to dedication in pursuit of their business and hobby. They are members in various antique oriented organizations, and have been advertising managers to an organization that promoted antique shows in various parts of the country.

Fred and Rose Booher maintain their present antique shop as well as their home, in an historic old home in Clinton, Missouri.

ACKNOWLEDGEMENTS

We wish to sincerely than our many friends in the field of antiques, both dealers and private collectors, who gave us their time, knowledge and understanding, as we gathered information for this book.

Please know we love you, we appreciate you and we thank you.

Fred and Rose Booher

INTRODUCTION

Graniteware has been called many names. Enamelware, enamel-ed ware, procelain and porcelainware are just a few. Granite cookware was introduced by the Lalance and Grosjean Manufacturing Company in Paris in 1878. The bright bold colors and attractive swirls and shades of the many patterns of granite ware were welcomed by housewives tired of the drab metallic colors of contemporary cooking utensils. The reaction to the new cookware was so favorable that hundreds of everyday items were produced in the enameled style from water pails to roasters and cuspidors, and everything imaginable in between.

Many manufacturers followed Lalance and Grosjean with their own line of granite cookware. Each producer had specific names for the lines and attractive labels and markings to immediately identify the brand of the utensil for the potential buyer. Lalance and Grosjean called their product "Agate Nickel-Steel Ware" and their label featured those words encircling "L&G MFG CO." Although it is not common to find old enamelware pieces still labeled with the original manufacturers label or mark, it is not impossible and these pieces, when found, mark the true treasures of the collectibles.

The Success Enameling & Stamping Company had many lines of graniteware. The "Dixie" line was a blue and white combination that used interlocking diamonds and a circle as a trademark. "White Diamond" was solid white with black edges and trim. The trademark for this line was a red circle with a diamond ring enclosed in a diamond. The words, "White Diamond Ware" appeared at the top. "Blue Diamond" was a high quality blue enamelware that carried the same trademark as "White Diamond" except in blue. A yellow circle surrounding a green four-leafed clover with the words "Shamrock Ware" identified the shaded green graniteware produced by the same company. The shaded purple variation carried a violet cirlce with green flowers and the words "Thistle Ware."

Other popular sellers of enamelware were Geuder, Paeschke and Frey Co., Hibbard Spencer Bartlett & Company, and The Belmont Stamping and Enameling Co. Hibbard Spencer Bartlett & Company sold four lines of graniteware. A grey mottled version was called "Chrysolite" and was marked by a yellow border around the trade name. A purple shaded design was called "Iris" and could be identified by a circle enclosing some irises and the brand. The "Nu-Blu" line was a light solid blue with dark trim. The trademark was a circle with "Nu-Blu" in the center. Rev-O-Noc was manufactured in a variety of colors and was marked by a red box with "Rev-O-Noc" inside. The Geuder, Paeschke and Frey Company sold a "Cream City" brand that was identified by those words in script. The Belmont Stamping and Enameling Company used the name on a banner covering a bell to label their product.

There were many more brands of enameled ware produced including Reed, Nesco Royal, Lafayette, Lisk, Ivorine, American White and White, Swedish and more. It would be impossible, however, to list and describe each type and label.

Some enamelware items leaned toward the ornate, and might be trimmed or decorated in wood, brass or pewter. One such decorated item we know of, is an old coffee pot with gooseneck pouring spout, wood handle trimmed in brass, and pewter lid. We also have an old kitchen shelf that is made with a cast iron backboard, black walnut shelf, and a brown and white enamelware towel bar.

Such items as the two described above are exceptional and will command a rather high price. (The coffee pot about $50.00; the shelf with enamelware towel rack $33.00.) Do not be too concerned if your collection contains few of the more ornate or unusual items. The old "garden variety" enamelware items make wonderful collections, and judging from the appeal of these old items, they will one day soon also be of high dollar value, such as the more ornate items.

Enamelware finish in many colors was extended to include old cast iron items. We have seen items such as iron boiling pots, old iron tea kettles and other cast iron items, that had a coating of enamel in swirl as well as in plain colors. These items are not as plentiful as the regular type enamelware that was produced. These items are worthwhile and are being collected today along with the other lighter weight enamelware items described.

The best advice we can offer the novice in judging whether a certain piece is "old" or new, or relatively new, is to obtain some old enamelware from a local reputable dealer and study the composition of the color designs. One rule of thumb is that most of the old and desirable items of enamelware - in any color - will be of a much heavier gauge metal than the newer, or present day items.

Granite was immediately very popular in the United States. It was sold primarily by mail order houses, hardware merchants and general goods stores. There are four basic patterns of enamelware

9

coloring: solid, shaded, swirled and mottled. The solid color is usually accented by a darker color trim. The swirl patterns usually have plain colored handles and trim. Purple, brown, and green shades are the most sought after colors of graniteware due to the relative scarcity of these colors. The most common color is white and many times is overlooked by the collector due to its great abundance. Grey mottled pieces are the second most common type of graniteware. This is the most collected type due to the easy location and the variety of pieces produced. Naturally, grey enamelware is less valuable than purple, brown or green.

Some graniteware items were manufactured with wire bails and wooden handles. These are considered to be premium pieces and generally demand higher prices. Repaired or damaged bails and handles will bring the price down on an otherwise high priced item. Many pieces have been chipped or cracked over the years. If the damage to the piece is minor to the overall appearance, or, if the item is unusual the value is not affected greatly. Still, graniteware items that are in good sound condition with no cracks or chips bring better prices on todays market.

Sweden, Austria, Germany and other European countries exported graniteware into the United States. Many of these foreign produced pieces have the country of origin stamped onto the bottom. Generally, foreign enamelware differs significantly in color from domestic pieces. More color is present and the colors have a brighter bolder hue than American graniteware.

Enameled ware pieces manufactured overseas also tend to be more heavily decorated than American pieces. We have on hand cups bearing raised animals in contrasting colors to the rest of the item. Of particular interest to us, is a two handled pink enamelware child's cup decorated with a red rim and a farm yard scene in color. A child with an egg basket is pictured in red, white, blue and brown. He is being chased by an attacking orange and white goose. There is a brown house and fence and brown landscape. This item was manufactured in Germany.

We also have a child's enameled pitcher 4¾" tall with a Dutch seaside scene on one side. The scene from Germany depicts a seated man smoking a pipe. He is wearing a red shirt, with a white collar, blue pants and black hat. The rim of the pitcher is blue or aqua. A girl seated on the edge of a boat is winding yarn. She is also very colorfully dressed. All of this appears on a white background. Naturally, these pieces that are heavily decorated and colorful are worth more than the simpler pieces.

The best place to find enameled ware is a farm or estate sale. Flea markets are also a good source. Early attendance of garage sales will also produce some interesting items. We have used our vacation time and miles to scour small out of the way towns, where there are junk shops or second hand stores.

Of particular interest to us is the decorating ability old enamelware has, especially the old colored swirl items. They lend a dash of color and nostalgia wherever placed. Nothing could be better in the decoration of the old country kitchen than these old enamelware items.

The prices shown in this book are average retail price per item, and are based on quotes from various antique dealers in America, and drawn from research and experience of the authors.

Prices quoted herein will have some variance depending on region or location of given item.

It would be impossible to give a price on some described item, and declare that price as absolute. The high and low figures given in this book are to establish a guide for the value of a given item.

GRANITEWARE LABELS

HIGH — GRADE ENAMELED WARE

12

COST SELL

CHRYSOLITE

HIBBARD SPENCER BARTLETT & CO
STATE STREET BRIDGE
CHICAGO

280

13½

517

8

20

NUBLU ENAMELED WARE

20

06

19

112

300, Roaster

30

ILLUSTRATION PLATE NO. 1

ROW 1 - LEFT TO RIGHT

1. Soap Dish with Integral Attaching Bracket,
   Overall Size 3" x 5½"..................... $ 5.00 - $ 9.00
2. Cream or Milk Dipper - 11" Handle......... $ 4.00 - $ 9.00

ROW 2 - LEFT TO RIGHT

1. Water Pitcher - 6 Qt. Capacity
2. Wash Basin - 4 Qt. Capacity

Commonly Called "Bowl and Pitcher Set" and Usually
Priced as a Set.............................. $18.00 - $24.00

ROW 3

Bread Dough Rising Pan. Has Footed Bowl, Domed
Lid with Perforations in Lid for Venting. 16½"
Diameter, 12" High.......................... $22.00 - $30.00

ILLUSTRATION PLATE NO. 2

ROW 1 - LEFT TO RIGHT
1. 1 Qt. Covered Baked Bean Pot . . . . $ 8.00 - $11.00
2. 6 Qt. Covered Stewing Pan . . . . $14.00 - $25.00

ROW 2 - LEFT TO RIGHT
1. Two Cooking Pots, 5 Qt. Capacity Each . . . . $ 5.00 - $10.00
2. Basting Spoon, 10" Handle . . . . $ 1.00 - $ 6.00

ROW 3 - LEFT TO RIGHT
1. Two Cooking Pots, 6 Qt. Capacity Each . . . . $ 8.00 - $12.00
2. Large Basting Spoon, 12" Handle. . . . . $ 1.00 - $ 6.00

ILLUSTRATION PLATE NO. 3

ROW 1 - LEFT TO RIGHT
1. Coffee Pot, 2½ Qt. Capacity . . . . $12.00 - $17.00
2. Coffee Pot, 2¾ Qt. Capacity . . . . $ 8.00 - $12.00

NOTE: Prices Shown Would Be For Coffee Pots With Lids.

ROW 2 - LEFT TO RIGHT
1. Coffee Pot, 2 Qt. Capacity . . . . $ 6.00 - $11.00
2. Goose Neck Pouring Spout Coffee Pot. Has Ornate
   Cast Iron Handle . . . . $12.00 - $20.00

ROW 3 - LEFT TO RIGHT
1. Coffee Pot, 8 Qt. Capacity . . . . $ 8.00 - $14.00
2. All White Coffee Pot, 12 Qt. Capacity . . . . . . $12.00 - $18.00

ROWS 1, 2 AND 3

These colanders are each a different shape and color and differ slightly in size. Colanders such as these would fall into the same price range with the greys falling into the low bracket and the blues falling into the higher bracket.

Colander.....................................$ 3.00 - $11.00

ROW 1 - LEFT TO RIGHT
1. Solid Color, Goose Neck Spout, 1 Cup
   Capacity Tea Pot ....$ 5.00 - $ 9.00
2. Tea Kettle, Whistle Spout. Made in England.
   2 Qt. Capacity............................$ 9.00 - $15.00

ROW 2
Heavy Cast Iron Coated with The Blue and White Enamel Swirl Pattern. Has Stylized Goose Neck Pouring Spout. Capacity of This Tea Kettle is 4 Quarts.

Tea Kettle....................................$25.00 - $35.00

ROW 3 - LEFT TO RIGHT
1. Tea Kettle. Goose Neck Spout. 3 Qt.
   Capacity ....$ 7.00 - $10.00
2. Tea Kettle. Goose Neck Spout. Has Flared
   Wire Bail. 2 Qt. Capacity ....$ 7.00 - $10.00

ILLUSTRATION PLATE NO. 6

ROW 1
Dish Pan, 17½" Diameter . . . . $ 9.00 - $16.00

ROW 2 - LEFT TO RIGHT
1. Wash Basin, 12" Diameter . . . . $ 6.00 - $ 8.00
2. Milk or Water Dipper, 13" Handle . . . . $ 5.00 - $ 9.00
3. Dish Pan, 16" Diameter . . . . $ 9.00 - $16.00

ROW 3 - LEFT TO RIGHT
1. Milk or Water Dipper, 12" Handle . . . . $ 5.00 - $ 9.00
2. Dish Pan, 18" Diameter . . . . $ 9.00 - $16.00

ILLUSTRATION PLATE NO. 7

ROW 1 - LEFT TO RIGHT
1. Cup and Saucer Combination . . . . $ 2.00 - $ 4.00
2. 10" Plate, Decorated Edge . . . . $ 1.00 - $ 2.00
3. Drinking Mug . . . . $ 3.00 - $ 5.00

ROW 2 - LEFT TO RIGHT
1. White Drinking Mug . . . . $ 2.00 - $ 4.00
2. "Cream Ware" Drinking Mug. . . . . $ 1.00 - $ 3.00
3. Blue and White Drinking Mug. . . . . $ 3.00 - $ 6.00
4. Yellow and White 12" Dinner Plate . . . . $ 6.00 - $12.00
5. Yellow and White Drinking Mug . . . . $ 5.00 - $10.00
6. Red and White 12" Dinner Plate . . . . $ 6.00 - $12.00
7. Red and White Drinking Mug . . . . $ 5.00 - $10.00

ROW 3 - LEFT TO RIGHT
1. Grey Drinking Cup. . . . . $ 1.00 - $ 2.00
2. Blue and White Drinking Cup . . . . $ 3.00 - $ 5.00
3. Mottled Pattern Drinking Cup . . . . $ 3.00 - $ 5.00
4. White 10" Plate . . . . $ 1.00 - $ 2.00
5. Blue and White Drinking Mug. . . . . $ 5.00 - $10.00
6. Blue and White 12" Dinner Plate. . . . . $ 5.00 - $10.00

ILLUSTRATION PLATE NO. 8

ROW 1 - LEFT TO RIGHT
1. Wash Basin, 11½" Diameter .... $ 6.00 - $ 8.00
2. Utility Bowl, 10" Diameter, 5" Deep .... $ 7.00 - $13.00

ROW 2 - LEFT TO RIGHT
1. Utility Pan, 8½" Diameter................. $ 1.00 - $ 3.00
2. Two Red and White Vegetable Bowls
   10" Diameter .... $ 7.00 - $13.00
3. Vegetable Bowl, 8" Diameter.............. $ 1.00 - $ 3.00

ROW 3 - LEFT TO RIGHT
1. Wash Basin, 12" Diameter .... $ 6.00 - $ 8.00
2. Shallow Utility Pan, 13" Diameter .... $ 4.00 - $ 7.00
3. Deep Utility Basin, 13½" Diameter........ $ 3.00 - $ 6.00

ILLUSTRATION PLATE NO. 9

ROW 1
Dish Pan, 14" Diameter . . . . $ 9.00 - $14.00

ROW 2 - LEFT TO RIGHT
1. Soap Dish, 3" x 5" . . . . $ 5.00 - $ 9.00
2. Chamber Pot, 13" Diameter . . . . $ 8.00 - $12.00
3. Soap Dish, 3" x 5½" . . . . $ 5.00 - $ 9.00

ROW 3 - LEFT TO RIGHT
1. Sick Room Bed Pan . . . . $ 3.00 - $ 6.00
2. Sick Room Utility Pan . . . . $ 4.00 - $ 8.00

ROW 1
Dish Pan, 17" Diameter . . . . $12.00 - $18.00

ROW 2 - LEFT TO RIGHT
1. Water Dipper. "Cream Ware" Brand.
   10" Handle . . . . $ 2.00 - $ 4.00
2. Dish Pan, 17½" Diameter . . . . $10.00 - $20.00
3. Water Dipper, 9" Handle . . . . $ 3.00 - $ 5.00

ROW 3 - LEFT TO RIGHT
1. Dish Pan, Shallow, 14½" Diameter . . . . $ 6.00 - $10.00
2. Dish Pan, 15" Diameter . . . . $ 6.00 - $10.00

ROW 1 - LEFT TO RIGHT
1. 14" Round Tray . . . .$ 4.00 - $ 8.00
2. 16" Oval Fish Platter . . . .$ 3.00 - $ 7.00

ROW 2
15" x 18" Solid Color Serving Tray . . . .$ 5.00 - $10.00

ROW 3 - LEFT TO RIGHT
1. 18" Diameter Serving Tray . . . .$19.00 - $28.00
2. 17" Oval Meat Tray. . . . .$ 6.00 - $10.00

ILLUSTRATION PLATE NO. 12

ROW 1 - LEFT TO RIGHT
1. 1½ Qt. Cooking Pot with Lid . . . . $ 5.00 - $10.00
2. Frying Pan, 10" with 10" Handle . . . . $ 3.00 - $10.00

ROW 2 - LEFT TO RIGHT
1. 2 Qt. Covered Cooking Pot . . . . $6.00 - $12.00
2. 2 Qt. Capacity Double Boiler . . . . $ 8.00 - $15.00
3. 1 Qt. Capacity Sauce Pan . . . . $ 6.00 - $11.00

ROW 3, LEFT TO RIGHT
1. Milk or Cream Ladle, 12" Handle . . . . $ 4.00 - $ 8.00
2. 2½ Qt. Cooking Pot . . . . $ 5.00 - $ 8.00
3. 1 Qt. Cooking Pot, Wire Bail and Pouring
   Spout . . . . $ 6.00 - $11.00

ILLUSTRATION PLATE NO. 13

These are all cake pans and pie pans, ranging in size from 9" to 11" in diameter.

Pans.. $ 1.00 - $ 6.00

ILLUSTRATION PLATE NO. 14

TOP TO BOTTOM, LEFT TO RIGHT

1. Oblong Photo Chemical Tray, 4" x 7"..... $ 3.00 - $ 5.00
2. Ale Bucket From Bavaria. Approximate Capacity is Less Than 1 Quart.................... $ 8.00 - $12.00
3. Small Cooking Pot. 1½ Pint Capacity ..... $ 4.00 - $ 8.00
4. Hot Plate Holding Item No. 3. 9" Diameter $ 3.00 - $ 6.00
5. Child's Play Mixing Bowl with Child's Eggbeater. Made in Sweden........................ $ 5.00 - $ 9.00
6. Handleless Tea Cup and Saucer, Small .... $ 1.00 - $ 3.00
7. Child's Drinking Mug .... $ 3.00 - $ 7.00
8. Two Handled Sugar Bowl, 3½" Diameter. . $ 7.00 - $14.00
9. Cereal or Berry Bowl, 4¼" Diameter ...... $ 4.00 - $ 7.00
10. Salesman's Sample Wash Basin, 3¼" Diameter.......................... $ 3.00 - $ 7.00
11. Small Cream Pitcher. Raised Seascape in Color on One Side .... $ 5.00 - $ 9.00
12. Child's Plate. Raised Figures in Center. 7½" Diameter.......................... $ 4.00 - $ 7.00
13. Child's Plate, Ornate Rim, Raised Figures in Center. 7½" Diameter.......................... $ 4.00 - $ 7.00
14. Small Utility Pan, 4" Diameter............ $ 2.00 - $ 4.00
15. Child's Doll House Cup and Saucer, Bowl and Drinking Mug. Size of Silver Dollar... $ 3.00 - $ 5.00 each
16. Child's Drinking Mug with Raised Figure of a Dog on One Side .... $ 5.00 - $ 9.00
17. Saucer, White on Top, Blue on Bottom, 5½" Diameter.......................... $ 1.00 - $ 3.00

ILLUSTRATION PLATE NO. 15

ROW 1
This 16" diameter basin is larger than the average for wash basins.

Wash Basin . . . . $ 5.00 - $10.00

ROW 2 - LEFT TO RIGHT
1. 10" Wash Basin . . . . $ 2.00 - $ 4.00
2. 12" Wash Basin . . . . $ 3.00 - $ 6.00

ROW 3 - LEFT TO RIGHT
1. 14" Wash Basin . . . . $ 3.00 - $ 7.00
2. 12" Wash Basin . . . . $ 3.00 - $ 6.00

ROW 1 - LEFT TO RIGHT
1. Water or Milk Dipper .... $ 4.00 - $ 9.00
2. Lidded Salt Box with Integral Attached
   Bracket.................................. $20.00 - $30.00

ROW 2 - LEFT TO RIGHT
1. Frying Pan, 10" Diameter, 10" Handle ..... $ 5.00 - $ 9.00
2. Frying Pan, 12" Diameter, 10" Handle ..... $ 7.00 - $11.00
3. Basting Spoon, Overall Length 15"......... $ 3.00 - $ 7.00
4. Basting Spoon, "Cream Ware" Brand,
   10" Handle .... $ 1.00 - $ 4.00
5. Spatula, 11" Handle .... $ 3.00 - $ 7.00

ROW 3
Baking Pan, Shallow, 10" x 14" .... $ 7.00 - $12.00

ROW 1 - LEFT TO RIGHT

1. Very Large Dipper Used To Transfer Milk or Cream From One Container to Another. Quart Bowl Capacity.............................$ 4.00 - $ 9.00
2. Standard Size Water or Milk Dipper........$ 3.00 - $ 8.00

ROW 2 - LEFT TO RIGHT

1. Dumpling Ladle, 12" Handle ....$ 4.00 - $ 7.00
2. Dumpling Ladle, 10" Handle ....$ 4.00 - $ 7.00
3. Utility Skimmer and Strainer ....$ 3.00 - $ 5.00
4. Basting Spoon...........................$ 1.00 - $ 6.00

ROW 3 - LEFT TO RIGHT

1. Shallow Ladle, 12" Handle ....$ 4.00 - $ 9.00
2. Round Bottom Cream Dipper, 10" Handle..$ 4.00 - $ 9.00
3. Water or Milk Dipper, 10" Handle ....$ 4.00 - $ 9.00

ROW 1 - LEFT TO RIGHT
1. Straight Sided 3 Gal. Utility Vessel . . . . $12.00 - $20.00
2. 6 Qt. Capacity Utility Bucket. . . . . $ 4.00 - $ 7.00

ROW 2 - LEFT TO RIGHT
1. Straight Sided, 2 Handled Utility Vessel . . . . $12.00 - $20.00
2. Milk or Cream Dipper, 10" Handle . . . . $ 1.00 - $ 3.00

ROW 3 - LEFT TO RIGHT
1. Two Milk or Water Pails, 3 Gal. Capacity . . . $12.00 - $20.00
2. Water Dipper, 12" Handle . . . . $ 4.00 - $ 8.00

ILLUSTRATION PLATE NO. 19

ROW 1 - LEFT TO RIGHT
1. Straight Sided 1 Gal. Capacity Colander
   With Wire Bail.......................... $ 9.00 - $14.00
2. Bottom Perforated, 3 Footed Colander ..... $ 3.00 - $ 7.00

ROW 2 - LEFT TO RIGHT
1. Dark, 3" Tea Strainer with Handle .... $ 4.00 - $ 8.00
2. Rounded Bottom Colander with Handle .... $ 3.00 - $ 6.00
3. Solid White 3" Tea Strainer with Handle.... $ 4.00 - $ 8.00
4. Colander with Circled Perforations........ $ 7.00 - $11.00
5. Two Handles, Footed Colander .... $ 7.00 - $11.00

ROW 3
Both colanders are 1 gallon capacity. The only difference being in the color configuration of the brown and white.

1. Colander................................. $ 9.00 - $14.00

ILLUSTRATION PLATE NO. 20

ROW 1 - LEFT TO RIGHT
1. Measuring Standard, 1 Pint Size .... $ 5.00 - $10.00
2. Measuring Standard, 2 Qt. Size .... $ 5.00 - $12.00
3. Measuring Standard, 1 Qt. Size .... $ 5.00 - $10.00

ROW 2 - HANGING LEFT TO RIGHT
1. Fruit Jar Filler Funnel.................... $ 4.00 - $ 9.00
2. Utility Funnel .... $ 4.00 - $ 9.00
3. Kerosene Lamp Filler Funnel .... $ 6.00 - $10.00

ROW 2 - SITTING LEFT TO RIGHT
1. Pudding Mold, Fluted Edges, Center
   Upright.................................. $ 4.00 - $ 8.00
2. Pudding Mold, Fluted Edges .... $ 4.00 - $ 8.00
3. Angel Food Cake Pan, Center Upright,
   10" Diameter .... $10.00 - $13.00

ROW 3 - LEFT TO RIGHT
1. Muffin Baking Pan, Holds 8 Muffins........ $ 8.00 - $12.00
2. Corn Bread Baking Pan, 7"x12" .... $ 2.00 - $ 5.00

ILLUSTRATION PLATE NO. 21

ROW 1
Covered Roasting Pan in 'Creamware" Brand.
22" x 10" .... $ 8.00 - $11.00

ROW 2
Covered Roasting Pan in the Blue and White.
22" x 10" .... $10.00 - $18.00

ROW 3 - LEFT TO RIGHT
1. Roasting Pan, 22" x 10". Lid is Nearly Flat
   with Indentations and Almost Recessed Lifting
   Handle .... $ 6.00 - $12.00
2. Small Covered Roasting Pan, 14" x 8" ..... $ 5.00 - $ 9.00

ROW 1 - LEFT TO RIGHT
1. Small Coffee Pot, 1/2 Qt. Capacity .... $ 9.00 - $12.00
2. Coffee Pot, 1 1/2 Gal. Capacity .... $10.00 - $15.00
3. Coffee Pot, 1 1/2 Qt. Capacity .... 8.00 - $12.00

ROW 2 - LEFT TO RIGHT
1. Brown and White Child's Mug .... $ 5.00 - $ 9.00
2. Coffee Pot, 2 Gal. Capacity .... $12.00 - $15.00
3. Brown Mug .... $ 4.00 - $ 8.00

ROW 3 - LEFT TO RIGHT
1. Coffee Pot, 1 1/2 Qt. Capacity .... $ 8.00 - $12.00
2. Coffee Pot, 1 3/4 Gal. Capacity .... $ 8.00 - $12.00
3. Coffee Pot, 2 Qt. Capacity .... $ 4.00 - $ 8.00

ILLUSTRATION PLATE NO. 23

ROW 1 - LEFT TO RIGHT
1. Pitcher, 1 Qt. Capacity . . . . $ 4.00 - $ 7.00
2. Advertising Pitcher . . . . $ 7.50 - $12.50
3. Cream Pitcher, 3/4 Qt. Capacity . . . . $ 3.00 - $ 6.00

ROW 2 - LEFT TO RIGHT
1. White Pitcher, 1 Gal. Capacity . . . . $ 8.00 - $15.00
2. Pitcher, White, black trim . . . . $ 8.00 - $15.00

ROW 3 - LEFT TO RIGHT
1. Pitcher, 3 1/2 Qt. Capacity . . . . $ 8.00 - $15.00
2. Pitcher, 4 1/2 Qt. Capacity . . . . $10.00 - $16.00
3. Pitcher, Blue and White . . . . $12.00 - $15.00

ADDITIONAL VALUES

1. Blue and white swirl gallon size tea kettle.............. $20. - 30.
2. Grey mottled gallon size tea kettle .... 8. - 15.

3. Blue and white swirl 10" high coffee pot.............. 12. - 17.
4. Grey mottled 10" high coffee pot .... 8. - 12.

5. Blue and white swirl 2 gallon size coffee pot .... 14. - 20.
6. Grey mottled 2 gallon size coffee pot................. 8. - 14.

7. Blue and white swirl 12" skillet...................... 5. - 12.
8. Grey mottled 12" skillet .... 3. - 10.

9. Blue and white swirl water dipper 10" handle.......... 5. - 10.
10. Grey mottled water dipper 10" handle .... 2. - 6.

11. Blue and white swirl drinking cup.................... 3. - 6.
12. Grey mottled drinking cup .... 1. - 4.

13. Blue and white swirl quart size double boiler.......... 8. - 15.
14. Grey mottled quart size double boiler .... 4. - 9.

15. Blue and white swirl 16" dish pan (2 handles) .... 10. - 20.
16. Grey mottled 16" dish pan (2 handles) .... 5. - 10.

17. Blue and white swirl 15" wash pan (no handles)........ 10. - 20.
18. Grey mottled 15" wash pan (no handles) .... 5. - 10.

19. Blue and white swirl 3 gallon size water or milk pail .... 12. - 20.
20. Grey mottled 3 gallon size water or milk pail.......... 5. - 12.

21. Blue and white swirl 10½" size colander .... 5. - 11.
22. Grey mottled 10½" size colander.................... 3. - 8.

23. Blue and white swirl chamber pot with lid.............. 20. - 30.
24. Grey mottled chamber pot with lid .... 5. - 12.

25. Blue and white swirl gallon size water or milk pitcher ... 8. - 15.
26. Grey mottled gallon size water or milk pitcher .... 5. - 10.

27. Blue and white swirl basting spoon .... 3. - 6.
28. Grey mottled basting spoon......................... 1. - 4.

29. Blue and white swirl ladle .... 4. - 8.
30. Grey mottled ladle .... 2. - 6.

31. Blue and white tea strainer (hard to find item).......... 6. - 12.
32. Grey mottled tea strainer (hard to find item) .... 4. - 8.

33. Blue and white swirl soap dish	$ 5. - 9.
34. Grey mottled soap dish	3. - 7.
35. Blue and white swirl muffin pan 6 cups	5. - 10.
36. Grey mottled muffin pan 6 cups	3. - 8.
37. Blue and white swirl muffin pan 12 cups	9. - 18.
38. Grey mottled muffin pan 12 cups	5. - 10.
39. Blue and white swirl bread pan	6. - 12.
40. Grey mottled bread pan	4. - 8.
41. Blue and white swirl sugar bowl (hard to find item)	7. - 14.
42. Grey mottled sugar bowl (hard to find item)	7. - 14.
43. Blue and white swirl pie plate 9" to 10"	2. - 5.
44. Grey mottled pie plate 9" to 10"	1. - 3.
45. Blue and white swirl cake pan 9" to 10"	2. - 5.
46. Grey mottled cake pan 9" to 10"	1. - 3.
47. Blue and white swirl pudding mold	6. - 12.
48. Grey mottled pudding mold	4. - 8.
49. Blue and white swirl spatula	5. - 8.
50. Grey mottled spatula	3. - 7.
51. Blue and white swirl hot plate	5. - 8.
52. Grey mottled hot plate	3. - 7.
53. Blue and white swirl sauce pan 8½"	5. - 10.
54. Grey mottled sauce pan 8½"	4. - 9.
55. Blue and white swirl roasting pan 20"	10. - 18.
56. Grey mottled roasting pan 20"	6. - 12.
57. Blue and white swirl roasting pan 16"	6. - 12.
58. Grey mottled roasting pan 16"	3. - 9.
59. Blue and white swirl lunch pail	7. - 12.
60. Grey mottled lunch pail	5. - 10.
61. Blue and white swirl scoop (hard to find item)	6. - 12.
62. Grey mottled scoop (hard to find item)	6. - 12.
63. Blue and white swirl child's cup	3. - 7.
64. Grey mottled child's cup	2. - 6.

65.	Blue and white swirl funnel............................	$ 6. - 12.
66.	Grey mottled funnel..................................	5. - 10.
67.	Blue and white swirl tea pot 5".......................	5. - 10.
68.	Grey mottled tea pot 5"..............................	4. - 9.
69.	Blue and white swirl dinner plate with partitions........	3. - 6.
70.	Grey mottled dinner plate with partitions..............	2. - 4.
71.	Blue and white swirl dinner plate plain................	3. - 5.
72.	Grey mottled dinner plate plain.......................	1. - 3.
73.	Blue and white swirl cup and saucer combination.......	4. - 7.
74.	Grey mottled cup and saucer combination.............	2. - 5.
75.	Blue and white swirl serving tray size 15"x20".........	12. - 18.
76.	Grey mottled serving tray size 15"x20"...............	10. - 15.

NOTE: Trays in the old enamelware came in many sizes, colors and color combinations. The larger trays are more valuable than the smaller ones in whatever color one finds them.

77.	Red enamel child's cup raised white dog 2½" high.....	5. - 9.
78.	Pink enamel child's mug, 2 handles, raised figure of child with eggs in basket, a goose pulling at child's pants..	6. - 10.
79.	White enamel child's pitcher with raised figure of Dutch boy and girl and boat 4" high.................	5. - 9.
80.	White enamel child's mixing bowl with beaters 2" high and 4¾" wide................................	5. - 9.
81.	White child's cereal bowl with raised figure of girl pushing doll in buggy, 8" wide......................	4. - 7.
82.	Blue and white swirl enamel child's cereal bowl with flowers in center, 8" wide..........................	4. - 7.
83.	Blue and white swirl enamel child's tea pot, 4" high....	5. - 9.
84.	Blue and white swirl child's enamel coffeepot 6" high...	6. - 10.
85.	Blue enamel cream pail 12" high.....................	8. - 12.
86.	White enamel cream pail 12" high....................	8. - 12.
87.	Grey enamel cream pail 12" high.....................	8. - 12.

88.	Salesman's sample white enamel wash pan............	$ 3. - 7.
89.	Salesman's sample blue and white swirl wash pan......	5. - 9.
90.	Salesman's sample blue and white swirl wash tub	5. - 9.
91.	Child's play dinner set - cups, saucers, plates, bowls (any color)...	20. - 30.
92.	Child's play table ware items, single pieces (any color)	1. - 5.
93.	Blue and white swirl serving platter 13" x 16"	12. - 18.
94.	Grey mottled serving platter..........................	3. - 8.
95.	Dust pan, any color (hard to find item)	8. - 15.
96.	Blue and white swirl measuring pitcher................	7. - 14.
97.	Grey mottled measuring pitcher	5. - 12.
98.	Blue and white swirl fruit jar filler funnel..............	5. - 8.
99.	Grey mottled fruit jar filler funnel	3. - 5.
100.	Grey mottled 2 gallon size steaming pot...............	4. - 8.
101.	Combination wall shelf with enamelware towel bar.....	30. - 35.
102.	Small two burner stove with enamelware top surface ...	12. - 18.
103.	Enamelware (any color or size) coffeepot with iron handle and goose neck spout........................	12. - 30.
104.	Any enamelware item any color, trimmed in wood, iron, pewter, brass or copper would be considered a very rare item and would command a price two or three times as much as a comparable item in plain enamelware.	
105.	Bread dough rising pan with lid, 12" high 16½" wide...	22. - 30.
106.	Baby bath tub, decorated with children and ABC's 30" long, 14" wide by 10" high. English..............	20. - 35.
107.	Blue and white swirl angelfood cake pan	10. - 15.
108.	Grey mottled angelfood cake pan.....................	5. - 10.

INDEX